With love T

Babu

22nd June 2012

CW00326585

the Leaves from Tree of Life

Sayings, Meditations and Prayers for a New Age

the Leaves from Tree of Life

Sayings, Meditations and Prayers for a New Age

As spoken by

Baba Dovid Yusuf

Compiled and Edited by David Heinemann

Sterling Paperbacks

STERLING PAPERBACKS
An imprint of
Sterling Publishers (P) Ltd.
A-59, Okhla Industrial Area, Phase-II,
New Delhi-110020.
Tel: 26387070, 26386209; Fax: 91-11-26383788
E-mail: sterlingpublishers@airtelmail.in
ghai@nde.vsnl.net.in
www.sterlingpublishers.com

Leaves from the Tree of Life
© 2007, Baba Dovid Yusuf
ISBN 978-81-207- 3350-3
Reprint 2008

Originally published by New Age Publications 1981
© The Rainbow Trust 1995

All rights are reserved.
No part of this publication may be reproduced, stored in a retrieval
system or transmitted, in any form or by any means, mechanical,
photocopying, recording or otherwise, without prior written
permission of the original publisher.

Based upon an original idea by Fatimah Nuradeen
Transcribed by *Nana* Layla Karman
Design & Artwork by David Heinemann
Additional Graphics by Avi Khalil

Printed and Published by Sterling Publishers Pvt. Ltd.,
New Delhi-110 020.

HOW TO USE THIS BOOK

In addition to using this book for devotional activities, special occasions and times of conflict or crisis, it can also be used to *answer questions,* or *give personal direction!* To use it for this purpose follow these steps:

1. Using key words, locate references in the **Index**.

2. Using the references discovered in the **Sayings** and the **Meditations** sections, contemplate on the meaning of these passages.

3. Say the *whole* meditation referred to out loud and as many times as necessary.

4. Using references found in the **Prayers** section, pray the whole prayer referred to silently and with serious intent.

5. Having done all the above, sit silently for at least 15 minutes, absorbing the spiritual incentives, answers, or guidance you receive.

6. Allow this guidance to modify your thinking and way of life.

7. *Be prepared for change, acting immediately where possible to implement the direction received!*

ACKNOWLEDGEMENTS

Bābā Dovid Yusuf (Babaji Sahib/Venerable Safa/Bro Francis/Rainbow Warrior/Prince the Friends/Shaykh al-Hāqq'anī, al-Uwaysī, al-Ja'farī, al-Chishti, al-Khwājagān an-Naqshbandī/Rabbi David Joseph) who gave permission for the publication of the limited edition, so making possible this general edition, acknowledged the countless hours spent on typing by Anna Betz, and all those who in various ways have made this publication possible.

It is published in honour of the saints of all religions and for the love of all the **Great Teachers:** Prophets, Masters, Messengers, Sages, Saviours, *Saoshyants, Avatars* and *Buddhas* - known and unknown - who have unselfishly served others. May peace and blessings be on them all without distinction and upon that Manifest Word of God whose life was a completion and perfection of their varied missions.

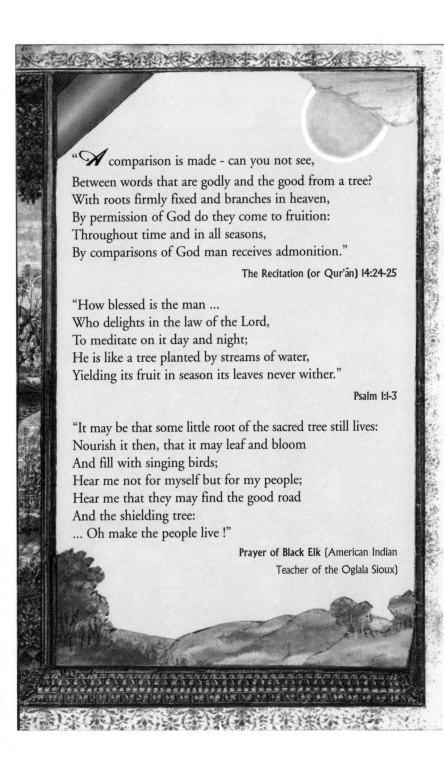

"A comparison is made - can you not see,
Between words that are godly and the good from a tree?
With roots firmly fixed and branches in heaven,
By permission of God do they come to fruition:
Throughout time and in all seasons,
By comparisons of God man receives admonition."

The Recitation (or Qur'ān) 14:24-25

"How blessed is the man ...
Who delights in the law of the Lord,
To meditate on it day and night;
He is like a tree planted by streams of water,
Yielding its fruit in season its leaves never wither."

Psalm 1:1-3

"It may be that some little root of the sacred tree still lives:
Nourish it then, that it may leaf and bloom
And fill with singing birds;
Hear me not for myself but for my people;
Hear me that they may find the good road
And the shielding tree:
... Oh make the people live !"

**Prayer of Black Elk (American Indian
Teacher of the Oglala Sioux)**

שְׁמַע יִשְׂרָאֵל, יְיָ אֱלֹהֵינוּ, יְיָ אֶחָד. سُورَةُ الْفَاتِحَة

παντων χρηματων ανθρωπος μετρον εστιν

諸供養具盛供養具供養最勝

PREFACE

This book represents in a very inadequate and limited form – a living expression of the *Eternal Truth,* which from time to time, is respoken by a living Master. When Baba spoke, the words were not his own, but those of the **Living Spirit** that spoke within and through him. When that happened it was evident to all, the difference between these words and those which as an ordinary man he used in everyday life.

Sometimes, Baba did not voice the words he heard (which were for him personally rather than others), but in appreciation for the direction he received responded by uttering an inspired and sung prayer as in the examples in the last section of the book. Unfortunately, it was not possible to reproduce the beautiful melodies he used to accompany these prayers.

We pray that this book will convey something of the spirit with which these words were spoken, but it cannot replace the experience of those who were able to be present on such occasions.

Many of the prayers used here are Baba's rendering of what was originally in Arabic, Hebrew, or some other language. They may not have been precise translations (except for those drawn from **The Recitation** or **Qur'ān**, and other Holy writings) but in all cases were an attempt to capture the real, intended meaning. A number of these prayers - like the meditations and sayings - are unique and were chanted, in response to questions, crisis situations, or at spiritual celebrations. Some of these prayers were written by others and adapted by Baba for his own use, but many of these prayers though in his own words, were attributed to others; e.g., pp 44, 58, 70, 73, 85, 92-95, etc., demonstrating his inspired ability to enter into the spirit of those for whom he spoke.

Baba was not a medium, nor did he ever claim to bring a new religion. His sole aim – as is also true for those who continue to speak for him – was to recognise unity amongst diversity; the One in all and the All in one. Though he spoke ahead of his time, his message is especially relevant today and recognition and implementation of the 3 Divine principles he propagated, is essential for our planet's survival.

IN THE NAME OF GOD, MOST KIND, MOST MERCIFUL

LIST OF ILLUSTRATIONS

Inside cover
From a medieval manuscript on Alchemy, showing Woman as a symbol of Divine Union with Nature (**Tree of Life**).

7-8
Death and Rebirth, illustrated by the destruction of the Amazonian Rain Forest.

45
Persian, Islamic fabric depicting the **Tree of Knowledge.** This becomes the **Tree of Life,** when the hidden aspects of the Cosmos are perceived through pursuit of the mystic path (*The Universal Way*).

101
From the **St. Louis Psalter** - Abraham ministering to three Divine messengers under a tree (the **Tree of Life,** see **Genesis 18:1-8**). A prophetic symbol of the three religions – *Judaism, Christianity* and *Islam* - which would arise from his descendants.

THE THREE PRINCIPLES

This book has been compiled by persons who though of different religious backgrounds and origins, are united in believing in the following three principles, which they believe are to be found at the heart of all genuine religious experience. They believe that these principles are inseparable and their recognition necessary, if there is to be peace with each other, with Nature & its Source, as well as within one's self.

1. The Unity and Sanctity of Life
2. The Oneness of the Human Family
3. The Common Basis of Religion

This book is based on these 3 principles.

INTRODUCTION

This book is a compilation on the subject of Life: its meaning, purpose, inner secrets and how it may best be lived.

SAYINGS

The sayings have been arranged in four sections corresponding to the seasons of the year and each contains twelve stanzas. They can therefore be used as weekly meditations.

Although they appear in almost the original form – with the exception of some minor grammatical changes – they represent a comprehensive view of teachings for a New Age. An age in which the teachings of all the world's religious founders can find their culmination, and in which a New World Civilisation can come into existence, founded upon the principles of justice, equality, tolerance and harmony. All over the world, individuals – knowingly or unknowingly – are responding to the spirit of a New Age and are working in different ways towards the birth of a New World Order.

Living as we do in a time of rapid change and unparalleled violence and conflict, humanity must come to see, that only if life is lived holistically (wholeness) and the interdependence of religion, politics and science accepted, can international, as well as personal peace be attained.

The sayings can generate thoughts which are contradictory to those stated, so that together they may create in the mind of the reader a new vision of life. From the destruction of previously limited thought patterns, the world can be seen in a new way: in a fresh and enlightened manner.

PRAYERS & MEDITATIONS

The highest form of prayer is silent communication with the Divine, when there is a total cessation of ego. It was during such states, that the Great Teachers had visions of past and future events. Receiving Guidance and Enlightenment that generated the unfolding of humanity's potential, triggering the next stage in the spiritual/social evolution of the planet and all its life forms.

We know of these communications through the records that the Great Teachers left. Some of these records were directly written down on papyrus, inscribed on leaves or clay, or chiselled in stone. In other cases where there was

no written language, or where the writing was inexact –
which is still true of some tribal peoples today – they were
transmitted in an oral form.

These teachers (Prophets, Masters, Avatars, etc.) also
left us with a record of their own thoughts and feelings as
they communicated with the source of all knowledge. We
call these entreaties *prayers* or *meditations*. Often others who
followed the teachings of the Enlightened Ones, were
themselves inspired to write their own prayers.

Coming at different times, in different parts of the
world – expressing each in an individual and unique way –
the Ultimate Source of Truth; all illustrated the underlying
Unity of Life and a common Source of Revelation.

Communication with the Source of Life, is the highest
form of communication possible and this requires that we
use the best form of expression available. Not necessarily
that of a literate kind, but words which truly express the
deepest feelings - the language of the heart. Often these are
to be found amongst the simple people of the world, who
although they may be lacking in literary education, are
superior in spiritual insight. They have inspired many of
the prayers included here. Prayers should be chanted, or
sung, whenever possible, but they should not be
accompanied by musical instruments for they are a direct
communication of the heart and should therefore be
expressed in a pure form.

Prayers said meaningfully – and not as a matter of
habit – are powerful in attaining desired ends. They are a
means of uplifting the spirit and of bringing us to a higher
and clearer perspective. The mind freed from preoccupation

with itself, can briefly glimpse the nature of Ultimate Reality and we are drawn closer to the Source of all that is.

The Eternal God of all humanity manifest to Christians and spoke to Hindus, Buddhists, Jews, Parsees, Muslims, Sikhs, etc. No nation or people, have been excluded from receiving guidance, for the Source of Truth is One, but it has many different expressions. Just as we are all human though of various skin colours and racial characteristics.

It is Our sincere wish that Arab and Jew; Black and White; East and West; come together in harmony and peace. * Each respecting and recognising the rights of the other and paying homage to the Beauty and Truth that is to be found in all cultures. May you too, look to that Source of Truth and Goodness who alone can bring world unity, putting an end to the horror of war and the misery of starvation.

19th February 1995/19th Adar 5755   **David Heinemann**
19th Ramadan 1415

* This prophetic promise by Baba, originally written in the first edition of this book, November 11th, 1981, awaits complete fulfilment.

REMEMBER

*O*h Child of dust and ashes

Do you not know that it was *I* who fashioned you!

Where were you when from a droplet you were moulded?
Were you your own creator in your mother's womb?
When your entombed within the earth shall *I* not see it?
Why then do you consider that your life is yours alone?

Do not control your affairs as if they were yours alone
For if you do then how can *I* take care of all your needs?
Can *I* be blamed for what occurs when you ignore my counsel?

Am *I* not there in All that is and all there is to know?

Before the count of Time you were within My mind
And after it has ceased your spirit shall remain with Me
In My Presence rest contented
As a child runs to its mother come to Me!

In the palm of my hand *I* shall lift you up
And bring you forward through all that you encounter
For am *I* not the Just Preserver!
Merciful, Compassionate, Creator and Destroyer?

I - alone - am the Eternal Friend!

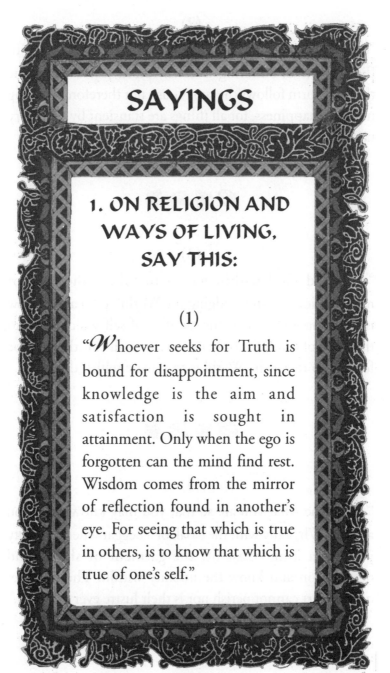

SAYINGS

1. ON RELIGION AND WAYS OF LIVING, SAY THIS:

(1)

"*W*hoever seeks for Truth is bound for disappointment, since knowledge is the aim and satisfaction is sought in attainment. Only when the ego is forgotten can the mind find rest. Wisdom comes from the mirror of reflection found in another's eye. For seeing that which is true in others, is to know that which is true of one's self."

(2)

"*K*now that tears chase laughter and goodness pain. In the shadow of suffering is often found joy. Even as the thunderstorm follows the sun. Grasp not therefore suffering nor even happiness, for all things are transient by their very nature. Freedom consists in accepting this as reality."

(3)

"*T*o find God within means to follow the path of renunciation. Acknowledging the World's pain and sorrow is renunciation. This is the sacrifice of self which leads to the Love of God, for only in service to all can the One be found. To reject the World is to pursue selfish desire."

(4)

"*B*ecome what you are so that you may know what you are not. Why tally with the cloak of a beggar when in reality you are a king? Cast off the garment of shame and degradation and know the nobility within. The treasures of the heart cannot perish nor is their lustre ever dimmed."

(5)

"*D*eny not hospitality, nor a gift, for this is not to allow others the pleasure of giving and is therefore the greatest meanness. But do not seek such offerings for there is no merit in compulsion, and one who gives out of expectation creates in himself and others a feeling of dissatisfaction."

(6)

"*S*ay what you mean and mean what you say: for your Self you cannot deceive and Life will call your insincerity to account. If you cannot trust yourself, how can others trust you?"

(7)

"*Y*ou have heard it said that you must love others as yourself; I say to you that if your love is so limited then it cannot be returned. Therefore, love others more than yourself and you will also be loved in such a way that the spark which you arouse in the heart of another will kindle that which is in your own heart."

(8)

"*The* Book of God is never closed, nor are its pages limited. Truth is One, but people give it different names. The colours of Autumn are but darker shades of Spring, and the snows of Winter, Summer's rain. So too, do I appear in every Age and every clime. Unless the trees were bare in Winter, they could not blossom in Spring. Birth and Death are One to Me and partiality the way of fools and arrogant mortals."

(9)

"*Worship* Me not as a man, nor offer Me what is already mine. I dwell in your innermost being and all things do I possess. Recognise that which is in the depth of your heart and you will see it in the hearts of others also. For I am the Source of all things: Mother and Father am I, the child and the unborn am I. This is worship for Me, that you see Me in all things and love all else as Me."

(10)

"*Submit* yourself to Me and you will find peace. Can the pot say to its maker, 'Why do you fashion me so?' Why then, Oh foolish being, do you imagine you can escape your Creator? Resistance is pain, anger is pride, and the wisdom of the intellect is foolishness to Me. Flow with My purpose and nothing that you do will ever be defeated. Reject My direction and sorrow, frustration and grief, will be your constant companion."

(11)

"The Lord of Life does not dwell in dead monuments or shrines that glorify the works of men, but in the secret places of the heart and in the wildness of natural things. Let first your body become a temple of light, even as the Christ did preach. Then let this light shine by works of love and service, so that the whole world becomes a temple for the Spirit of the Eternal One."

(12)

"To grasp happiness is to kill joy, and to seek pleasure is to find pain. Contemplate the wisdom of your Lord that you may see your emptiness. Only when the self is dead can the reality of the Eternal Self be seen. Be content in whatever state you find yourself, that your prayerful and meditative attitude of mind, may allow you to share the burden of others. This is the true love of Self."

II. ON POLITICS, ECONOMICS AND GOVERNMENT, SPEAK:

(1)

"*R*iches depend on the existence of poverty, and as long as poverty exists there can never be world peace. Consequently, wealth and war are interdependent, and poverty and peace are mutually exclusive."

(2)

"*N*o law is there greater than justice, no knowledge clearer than truth. The basis of all justice is mercy, and the origin of truth righteousness. Without religion how can there be mercy? Know then that all authority comes from natural law, and all life from its Source. Whosoever creates a law that contravenes the law of life must be resisted. This is just, honest and a duty – to all that is – both past, present and future."

(3)

"*F*rom the destruction of a tree paper is made, but the lines on its bark are more majestic than a thousand books. Seek greatness in little things and power in humility, for arrogance will be defeated and pride turned into foolishness."

(4)

"*We* are born owning nothing but the necessity for love, and we die leaving nothing but sorrow. Therefore, share goodness with others and deny not anyone that which belongs to all. For the fruits of the earth are entrusted to everyone, and whoever seeks to possess them is a thief creating murder and evil."

(5)

"*Do* not lend or borrow, for money is time. Your life cannot be given to another nor can it be purchased. Give freely without thought of return and you also will receive when you have need."

(6)

"*Prosperity* obtained by hard work is meritorious. Prosperity obtained by creating poverty is an abomination. Those who pile up wealth beyond their needs establish evil. To obtain wealth by interest is to profit from poverty. Riches obtained without working are not earned and are therefore stolen. This is the cause of misery, envy, crime and injustice."

(7)

"Say: the world is my country and my family its citizens. All men are my brothers, and all women I honour as my mother. No colour, culture, or creed, do I omit from the Divine, for all spring from the same Source."

(8)

"Peace cannot come from conflict, nor can life come from death. The violence of parents against their children sows the seeds of strife and discontent. So too will the aggressive Nation be resisted with bloodshed and will in turn become the vanquished and defeated."

(9)

"I make the sun shine upon all humanity and the seas of rain are shared by all. Each is born and each must die, and food is sought by everyone. Who then can draw a line upon My Earth? Whose needs are greater than another? No Nation is more glorious in My eyes, and no people more superior to Me, than those which see themselves as equal to the rest. The path of National Pride is presumption and folly and leads to violence and death."

(10)

"War is an abomination, peace can never come from strife. Whoever fights in one war lays the foundation for another; the land that is preserved by blood will in blood be taken. To die for others is the greatest good, but to kill for others is the greatest evil."

(11)

"You have heard it said: 'Love your enemies and do good to those who hate you.' I say unto you, let no one be your enemy and everyone your friend. Make no distinction between your family and friends, nor even between yourselves and those of another nation. For the Lord loves all equally, and no race or nation does the Source consider greater."

(12)

"Submit yourselves, Oh Nations, to My will, that you may know peace. For I control all, am in all, and are of all. Though nations rise and fall, My constancy remains. Emperors and Kings have fallen, and great Orators are soon forgotten, but those who speak My words live on and never die. Civilisations come and go, but Truth remains for ever. More powerful than an army is a true word quietly spoken."

III. ON SCIENCE, KNOWLEDGE AND THE STRUCTURE OF THINGS, SAY:

(1)

"*I*mmerse yourselves in the Ocean of My words that you may find eternal bliss. Transient are the works of men, but My knowledge shall never cease. Those who seek therein will find the Source of all mysteries and truth. Wonder and honour shall be conferred upon them."

(2)

"*T*he Source of all things is their end, for the end is the beginning. Therefore, did the Son of Man say, 'Before Abraham was I AM.' This is the secret mystery of the Universe that holds the key to all science."

(3)

"*A*n unjust thought harboured within the soul will cause disease. Envy, spite, malice and ill-will disturb the mind, bringing sickness to the heart. Jealousy, resentment and anger, damage the liver and the spleen. Hate, attachment and denial, bring misery and permanent despair that makes the spirit low. False-face covers loss, and the pride of self-sacrifice grows within, manifesting throughout the body. Be balanced in your ways and thoughts, that the Spirit of Wholeness may radiate in your life and in your flesh."

(4)

"A glass may be half-full or half-empty: every positive thought has a negative aspect, and every negative quality something positive within it. The death of a seed is the birth of a flower, and the death of a flower the birth of a seed. The Universe we perceive is the Universe our minds create."

(5)

"The ways of humanity are not the Way of Nature. Humankind seeks to perpetuate that which is mortal, but Nature creates from destruction. Give yourself to Me that I may create a new being from the fragments of the old. Submit to My direction and know contentment. Resistance is pain, acceptance is joy. A child is born in blood."

(6)

"Glory not in what you attain, nor seek your satisfaction in empty things, for the honours that men confer are as foolishness in the eyes of Time. Life and dignity reside in all, how then can it be given? Progress in knowledge comes from those who disregard convention, fashion and the orthodox."

(7)

"From the rubbing together of two sticks is fire made. Flesh, in friction with flesh, produces a spark of life from which a child is born. The clash of steel on stone, brings sharpness to a knife. Conflict of opinion produces clarity and seeds of thought. Thus is knowledge born."

(8)

"To listen often is to learn, to speak often is to be ignorant. Let your words be few and your deeds be many. The shallow brook causes a ripple, but still waters run deep. Be open to the opinions of all that sincerity may be effected. Knowledge that is genuine can be examined, but sham truth will not stand up to scrutiny."

(9)

"A rose though pleasant in smell is sharp with thorns. The lion purrs like the cat but its claws mete out death. The whale is Nature's giant, but flesh it does not tear. The moon though brightly lit has no light of its own. Appearance is not reality: do not trust your senses, nor believe in what you see. Truth is incontestable, so can't be known with finite minds, hence knowledge always increases."

(10)

"As black needs white and darkness is known through light, so am I created by My image. For all that is, there is an opposite that turned upon itself reflects. Thought becomes action and action becomes thought; dream becomes reality and reality a dream of past events. Knowing this accept what is, using good and evil for transcendent ends. Let not your action be to right or left, but find the middle-way, for this is Nature's path."

(11)

"For each cause there is effect and for each effect a cause. What then is cause and what effect? Who is the Creator and who the created? Can energy be known without form? The chicken needs the egg for it to be born, but the egg needs the chicken in order for it to exist. Why then do you separate yourselves from Me, am I not your own True Self?"

(12)

"Oh foolish beings, why do you seek a life of ease and pleasure? Can the tree grow without pushing its way through the soil? Or the fish swim without the restriction of water? When Mother Earth is plundered, Her children suffer. Without movement there is no life, and without effort there is no reward. To feel no pain and be at constant ease is death. Fight against Me and you will be defeated. Work with Me and you will have success. Destroy My earth and it will destroy you. Run with the wind and you will find exhilaration."

IV. ON DEATH, ITS MEANING AND MYSTERY, STATE:

(1)

"*W*ithout night there could be no dreams, and without death there could be no life. How could there be birth without old age, or how could we know joy without pain? Is not the childhood of old age even as that of youth? Why then do you distinguish between birth and death? Life is a dream and death an illusion."

(2)

"*D*o not exalt yourself over others, nor rejoice overmuch in your good fortune. For you too are the food of worms and at death will be found to be equal."

(3)

"*K*now this, Oh Son of Woman, that Life is but a journey and Death is at its end. Can you travel without knowing your destination and be sure of the best route? Focus on your destiny and you will find the path to travel. The purpose of Life is Death and to ignore your destination is to be lost in a fog of illusion."

(4)

"*The* Kingdom of Heaven is like a mustard seed that planted in good soil brings forth a useful plant. Right thoughts implanted in the heart give rise to useful works; but wrong thinking produces rotten fruit that putrefies. Perform right works and you will know right thoughts: the Paradise thus attained cannot be taken from you and will remain even when the body decomposes."

(5)

"*As* the rim of the wheel that has no end, so is the cycle of existence for one confined to Hell. The place of burning torment where satisfaction can never be attained, and pain and suffering do not cease. Greed consumes like fire, and the desire to attain power leads to frustration. Anguish and torment, are companions to anxiety and fear, for those who know this place. This world is Hell if no other world do we perceive. Confined to seeking pleasure from a transient place, we shall ever wander as ghosts in a limbo of existence."

(6)

"*O*bserve your Self in the mirror of your mind. Reflect upon that which existed before you were born and will continue to exist even after your death. Detached, become One with that which destroys and creates in the same moment. Knowing this you will know all there is to know: You as your own creation and your own dissolution. Attach not yourself to the impermanent 'I', for this is illusion and the source of all sorrow."

(7)

"*W*ork not for the future, or cling on to the past: nothing but change is constant. Future never comes and past prevents the present manifesting. Those who know this live within the present, watching, while the ghosts of others live in their dreams of past and future."

(8)

"*D*eny not what is, nor try to create what cannot be. The fool lives in yesterday only to suffer on the morrow. Live each day as though it were your last, and death will not catch you unawares. Whatever your hand finds to do, do this with all your might. Never again will this moment come and regrets cannot return lost time. Change what you can, but accept what you can't; consider not the unchangeable for this leads to frustration and grief."

(9)

"At birth you are alone struggling to be born. At death you are alone watching your life ebb away. Grasp not at others nor seek refuge in a mortal being, for death will shake you from your dreams. Consider your aloneness and you will find an inner strength that you can share with others."

(10)

"Listen to the stillness that resides within your Being. Meditate upon the quietness that dwells within your heart. Know the sound that silence makes and you will see your Self. The Self that dwells in all and knows no death. At that moment you will know the past and future as One, absorbed within the present. This is Consciousness; that which sees not end or beginning."

(11)

"You have heard it said, the sins of the fathers are visited upon the children, or wrong action produces bad effects. As pleasure follows pain, so does the Mercy of God bring an end to the suffering of little children, for this is just. The measure of sorrow inflicted upon parents, is equal to their denial of a future life."

"Think of the spring when drinking its water. At what point does a raindrop become a river, or when does the river become the sea? Know then that the Source is in all things, and all things are from the Source. Why then by selfishness do you separate yourselves from Me? This is the cause of all pain and suffering."

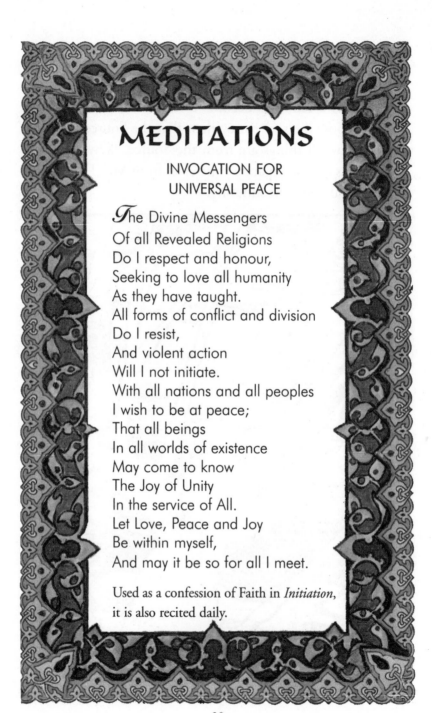

MEDITATIONS

INVOCATION FOR
UNIVERSAL PEACE

The Divine Messengers
Of all Revealed Religions
Do I respect and honour,
Seeking to love all humanity
As they have taught.
All forms of conflict and division
Do I resist,
And violent action
Will I not initiate.
With all nations and all peoples
I wish to be at peace;
That all beings
In all worlds of existence
May come to know
The Joy of Unity
In the service of All.
Let Love, Peace and Joy
Be within myself,
And may it be so for all I meet.

Used as a confession of Faith in *Initiation*,
it is also recited daily.

A CHRISTIAN DEVOTIONAL MEDITATION*

May my heart be a church for Your worship,
May my words become Your song,
May You always dwell within me,
     every day and all day long.

May my eyes behold Your Glory,
May my breath take You in,
May You always be with me,
     to deliver me from sin.

May my ears hear Your whispers,
     as you watch me sleep,

May I always see the Path,
     You have lighted for my feet.

May You grant me Your Peace,
     as Your wishes I convey to others,

May I regard any stranger as my sister,
     or my brother.

May I always love You,
     and obey all Your commands,

May You always be my saviour,
     who forever holds my hand.

* Adapted from a traditional Filipino prayer.

MEDITATION FOR PEACE

Baba recommends this as a group meditation, particularly in times and places of conflict, war, or disturbance. It is recited by a leader of meditation and meditated upon by the group as a whole. Allow approximately a minute between each item.

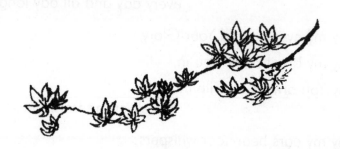

We use this space and time to meditate. One by one, we meditate on each item as mentioned, giving our energy and thought to what is said. Completely absorbed in the moment of quietness, self is forgotten and discarded and replaced by a positive transmission of Peace and Love.

ॐ ॐ ॐ

To those who are nearest and dearest to us,
We send out thoughts of Love:
On this we meditate.

All those who have offended or irritated us,
We think of one by one and send out thoughts of Love:
On this we meditate.

❦❦❦

To all those who are indifferent to us,
We send out thoughts of affection and Love:
On this we meditate.

❦❦❦

To our enemies known and unknown,
We send out thoughts of affection and Love:
On this we meditate.

❦❦❦

To all World Leaders bent on sorrow,
Destruction and on grief,
We send out thoughts that they may learn to Love:
On this we meditate.

❦❦❦

To all nationalities, cultures, creeds
And colours of the skin,
We send out thoughts of Love:
On this we meditate.

❦❦❦

To all creatures great and small,
In all worlds of existence,
We send out thoughts of Love:
On this we meditate.

❦❦❦

Passing flights of fancy and of whim based on
The satisfaction of desire, we now reject:
On this we meditate.

❦❦❦

In place of personal gain we give respect,
Sincerity of heart drives out all thoughts of hate:
On this we meditate.

❦❦❦

Ill-will no longer is our Master,
As anger disappears so do all violent thoughts:
On this we meditate.

Learning to Love all else, we also Love our Self;
For in our innermost Being, is that which makes us One;
All within all worlds existing,
Indestructible, Undefeatable and Eternal:
On this we meditate.

May our inner Peace
Become the Peace of all we meet,
May its radiance be felt throughout the world:
On this we meditate.

May our meditation become our thoughts;
May our thoughts become our actions:
So be it!

MEDITATION FOR RELIGIOUS AND RACIAL HARMONY

This meditation is recommended for times or places of religious strife or racial conflict. Recited by a leader of meditation and then meditated upon by the group as a whole, allow approximately a minute between each item. Alternatively, it may be recited in unison. It can also be used in conjunction with Hindu *Jappa*, Muslim *Misbāhāh*, or Christian *Rosary* beads, in individual meditation.

*T*o the Most Kind, All Compassionate,

Source of Harmony, Peace and Love;

We/I recite these verses.

🌸🌸🌸

For the manifestation of Life in all its forms

Both great and small,

In all worlds of existence;

We/I recite these verses.

🌸🌸🌸

For the Cycle of Existence
And the knowledge of the place from which we/I came
And to where we/I shall return;
We/I now give thanks.

For Adam the father of all women
And Eve the mother of all men;
We/I now give thanks.

For all nationalities, colours of the skin
And varieties of culture;
We/I now give thanks.

For all doors to Truth, known and unknown,
And those who have spoken for Truth
Through their way of life;
We/I now give thanks.

For Prophet Abraham, who left his home,
His family and his country, to found a greater family:
To discover a larger world
And a homeland for Arab and for Jew;
We/I now give thanks.

❧❧❧

For Moses, a shepherd of men,
A prophet for Muslims, for Christians, and for Jews;
We/I now give thanks.

❧❧❧

For Zarathustra's purity of intention,
His zeal for justice and for right;
We/I now give thanks.

❧❧❧

For the wisdom of Confucius
And the Way of Lao-Tsu;
We/I now give thanks.

❧❧❧

For Krishna's joy of living
And the devotion of Radha – his wife;
We/I now give thanks.

❦❦❦

For the Enlightened One's compassion
And his noble path of peace;
We/I now give thanks.

❦❦❦

For the humanity of Israel's Jesus
And the motherhood of Mary;
We/I now give thanks.

❦❦❦

For the Prophet Muhammad's dedication
As God's messenger of Unity;
We/I now give thanks.

❦❦❦

For the courage and the fearlessness,
Of Guru Nanak and his followers;
We/I now give thanks.

For the Bab, who sacrificed his life
As a gateway to the New Age;
We/I now give thanks.

❀❀❀

For Baba, who has taught the Universal Way
To seek God within ourselves,
Within all beings and each other;
We/I now give thanks.

❀❀❀

For the saints of all religions
And the men and women of all cultures,
Of different creeds and colours of the skin;
Those who served unselfishly their fellow human beings;
We/I now give thanks.

❀❀❀

(Return to the first verse repeating the whole as many times
as necessary.)

MEDITATION FOR A CHRISTIAN FRIEND SEEKING GUIDANCE

Oh Wayfarer that stands upon the shores of Destiny
where past and future meet,
Think not that the Ocean of His Grace
can fail to satisfy your need,
But travel thereupon to distant lands whose sounds
and scents are far removed from whence you stand.

Know then that every channel has a path and
every river runs into the Sea to lose its individuality,
Check your heart from flowing outwards into sands
of Time where winds of Fate blow every trace away,
But inwards to the inner light flow onwards to the
Way where is the Ocean of Eternal Light.

From this Majestic Sea comes every form of life
to manifest an outward form that mirrors an Infinity,
For does not the voice of God resound in every heart?
– as speaking to Muhammad says:
"I am the Light of heavens and of earth"*
and of every stage and station on the Path.

*The Recitation 24:35

41

MEDITATION FOR A MUSLIM FRIEND WHO DISCOUNTS SUFIS

Oh my brother:

> Burn the Book so that you may discover the
>
> Revelation of God within your heart!

Oh my brother:

> Turn your back on Mecca and you will know
>
> That Allāh can be found in every place!

Oh my brother:

> Leave country, tradition and respect, and
>
> Follow in the Prophet's path!

MEDITATION FOR A DRUG ADDICT
SEEKING GUIDANCE

*W*hat is passion but a search for Him?

In Union we find ecstatic bliss!

The pain of separation can't be dulled

By drugs, or dreams, or drink,

Until we find our self submerged in Him

We cannot find relief!

MEDITATION FOR A SEEKER EXPERIENCING MARITAL DIFFICULTIES*

*W*hat is love if it does not overwhelm us,

Surround us and engulf us?

Can there be love without surrender,

Or fire without a flame?

Oh seeker of the Beloved bare your bosom,

That the Doorkeeper of the heart

May enter and beat within!

EVENING MEDITATION

This meditation is chanted nine times by Baba and his followers when retiring to bed at night.

*O*h Source of Life,

That knows the secrets of my heart,

Reveal unto me the innermost depths of my being;

That in knowing my Self,

I may know You also.

*Inspired by the prayers of the female Sufi Saint, Rābi'ah al-'Adwiyya of Basra, Iraq (died 801).

45

PRAYERS

"Bismillāh-ir-Rahmān-ir-Raheem

al-hamdu li-Lāhi Rabbi-l-'Alameen

ar-Rahmān-ir-Raheem

Māliki yowmi-d-deen

Eyāka na'budu wa'eyāka nastaeen

Ihdinā 'ssirāta-l-mustakeem

مِنْ إِلَى الَّذِينَ أَنْعَمْتَ عَلَيْهِمْ غَيْرِ

Sirāta-llezeena 'an'amta 'aleihim,

الْمَغْضُوبِ عَلَيْهِمْ وَلَا الضَّالِّينَ

*Gheiri-'l mughdoobi 'aleihim
walā-dsaaleen."*

The Recitation 1:1-7

Here is Baba's rendering of the Arabic:

"In the Name of God,

Most Kind, Most Merciful.

Praise be to THE God who is Lord of the worlds:

Most Kind, Most Merciful,

Ruler of the Day of Reckoning.

You alone do we worship;

You alone do we implore for help.

Guide us along the straight Path:

The Way of those whom You have blessed:

Not of those who are chastised by Your anger,

Nor of those who are wandering astray."

Baba often used the above Arabic invocation as a preliminary to prayer, meditation, healing or guidance. It was revealed by God to the Prophet Muhammad for this purpose: see The Recitation 15:87.

47

PRAYER FOR RITUAL PURIFICATION

This prayer is used while performing ablutions with water – or clean earth or sand, if water is not available – before declaring as a believer, communal prayer, or on any other occasion when it is desired to cleanse the mind and body from unjust, impure, or violent intentions.

Holding the water in the palms of the hands, you say:

'Bismillāh-ir-Rahmān-ir-Raheem.'
Oh Source from whom all life does spring,
To you my body, mind and thoughts, I bring.

Then rubbing the water between the fingers and washing the hands to the wrists, beginning with the right hand (symbolic of deliberate intention), you say:

Oh cleanse my hands from taking
what does not belong to me,
From theft and violence, greed and usury.

Then washing out the mouth three times (symbolic of emphasis and completeness), you say:

Oh God Almighty cleanse my mouth
and purify my tongue,
From lies, deceit, flattering and foul speech,
or angrily committing wrong.

Then washing out the nose three times, say:

Oh God Almighty as I wash my nose, make my nostrils clean,
from the stench of bigotry, of war and every impure thing.

Then washing the face with the palms of the hands three times, you say:

Eternal One, You have said: "All else perishes except My face", *
So wash away my outer self, that all may see your inner Grace.

Then washing the arms up to the elbows three times, beginning with the right, you say:

Strengthen my arms Oh Lord, that I may help in carrying the burden of others;
Cleansed from embracing power or wealth, to see all persons as sisters and as brothers.

Then washing the neck and ears, you say:

Oh Beloved cleanse my ears that I may hear what you have said,
In the writing on my heart, in Nature and the many Holy Books I've read.

Then wiping all over the top of the head with wet palms, you say:

Oh Blessed Source, descend and purify my actions and my thoughts.

Then washing each foot and ankle three times, beginning with the right, you say:

Direct and Guide my steps that I may walk upright and true -
'lāilāha illā-Llāh'-
There is no God but You!

*The Recitation 55:26-27

A PRAYER FOR TRAVELLING *

May it be Your Will,
Oh Lord my God and God of my fathers,
To lead me safely and in peace.

Bring me to my destination joyfully,
Delivering me, Oh my Lord,
From all enemies and every form of danger.

Send Your blessings upon all I do,
And let Your Graciousness, Kindness and Love,
Be found in the eyes of those I meet.

Listen to all I implore from You,
Oh God who hears all prayers,
Pay attention to my plea for peace.

For You are the Blessed One,
The Lord who hears my voice.
The God who heeds a prayer.

* Adapted from a traditional Jewish prayer, Baba urged that it be used in times and places of anger and terrorism.

PRAYER FOR THE NEW AGE

Lead me ...

> From darkness to Light

Lead me ...

> From sickness to Health

Lead me ...

> From suffering to Joy

Lead me ...

> From ignorance to Truth

Lead me ...

> From death to Life

Lead me ...

> From hate to Love

Lead me ...

> From self to Service.

This Vedic prayer is chanted & used with appropriate steps.

THE SONG OF LOVE

Come Bird of Paradise
And I will fly with you
Freed from the prison of self I will fly
Fly in the Heaven of God!

Released from my bondage
Detached from thoughts of gain
I will fly above the conflict
But live within the pain
Vision clear I know my goal
My flight is straight and true
Come Bird of Paradise
And I will fly with you
Freed from the prison of self I will fly
Fly in the Heaven of God!

With my Beloved the melody of Unity we sing
The Oneness of All is the message that we bring
Harmony's been planted
The Harvest is now due
Come Bird of Paradise
And I will fly with you
Freed from the prison of self I will fly
Fly in the Heaven of God!

Singing the song of Love

The spirit soars within my breast

The branches of the Tree of Life

Have spread from East to West

Perched upon its branches

We'll find eternal peace and rest

Come Bird of Paradise

And I will fly with you

Freed from the prison of self I will fly

Fly in the Heaven of God!

Come Bird of Paradise

And I will fly with you

Freed from the prison of self I will fly

Fly in the Paradise of Love

Fly in the Paradise of Love

Fly in the Heaven of God!

PRAYER FOR LOVING KINDNESS *

May I be happy,

May I be free from misery,

May I be free from enmity,

May I be free from ill-will,

May I be free from suffering,

May I be well and happy :

May all beings be free from enmity,

May all beings be free from ill-will,

May all beings be free from suffering,

May all beings remain within their happiness.

(Pali)

Aham Sukhito homi,

Aham Nidukkho homi,

Aham Avero homi,

Aham Abyahpajjho homi,

Aham Anigo homi,

Sukhi Attanam Pariharami:

Sabbe Satta Avera hontu,

Sabbe Satta Aryapajjha hontu,

Sabbe Satta Anigha hontu,

Sabbe Satta Sukhi Attanam Pariharantu.

* Traditional Buddhist chant.

PRAYER TO OPEN THE HEART

Source of Love of Life and Being
Enter now into my heart
Give me Peace and give me Guidance
Let my sorrows all depart
Into the gloom despair and conflict
Bring Your Light of faith and hope
Guide me always ever closer
To Your Kingdom in my heart
Take away all fears and anguish
Lift my burden and my grief
Give me sight to see Your Power
Vision clear detached from all
For You are bliss and true contentment
Loving Self and loving all.

PRAYER FOR GUIDANCE *

Oh Lord, in Mercy grant my soul to live,
And patience grant, that hurt I may not grieve:
How shall I know what thing is best to seek?
You only know and what You know please give!

* 'Abd Allāh Abu Ismā'īl al- 'Ansrārī, the Sufi (died 1089).

PRAYER FOR UNDERSTANDING *

A seeking, a searching:

To seek whither,

To search the land,

To seek the origin;

To seek the root,

To seek out the base,

To search the unknown,

To seek out the Spirit of things:

May it be effectual!

* Based on a native Maori (of New Zealand) prayer.

PRAYER FOR TRANQUILLITY *

Oh my Lord:
Never do I listen to
The voices of the animals,
The rustling of the trees,
The splashing of the waters,
The songs of the birds,
The whistling of the wind,
The rumbling of the thunder,
But that I sense in them Your Unity.

You are beyond comparison:
You are Incomparable,
You are Ever Prevailing,
You are the All knowing.
You are the All Wise,
You are the Ever Just,
You are the Whole of Truth,
Without defeat, ignorance, foolishness, injustice, or falsehood.

Oh my God:
I acknowledge Your Presence
In that which You have created,
The Evidence of Your Existence
In Your each and every Act,
Grant me, I pray, that my satisfaction,
Be only found in Your satisfaction,
My remembrance of You
In my Love for You;
That my delight shall be
As that of a father for his child,
Let my resolve be firmly fixed
Within Your serenity and tranquillity.

* Based on a prayer of Dhu-n-Nun Misrī, an Egyptian Sufi
(died 860). Baba used this prayer when visiting places of
natural beauty; forest, moorland, mountain or desert.

PRAYER FOR OVERCOMING DISTRESS *

Oh You who are Beloved,
This pledge to You I vow :
Though pain of separation
Has torn my heart asunder,
Yet never will I cease to
Contemplate Your Beauty,
Nor ever wish to be aught
But the slave-girl of Your heart.
Oh Master and my Lord!
You know what lies within me,
My body burns in ecstasy of
Your Love within my heart
Can I ever be disgraced when
You have chosen me as Lover?
Our wedding-union garment
Displayed for all to see!
This world is but a prison
That Your Love has freed me from,
Through love of You
My sorrows become a remedy:
You, Oh You! who art my soul's
Sole Source of satisfaction!
Remove ingratitude for
Your gift of difficulties.
You are the very essence
Of all for which I yearned,
The vision of Your Oneness
Has blinded me with love:
To the world I am a stranger
From their lists of Saints excluded,
But You're my Friend and constant Lover,
Whose acceptance shall not cease.

* Inspired by Tufah (died 856), a Sufi minstrel slave-girl
imprisoned by her Master for ecstatic utterances.

HEALING PRAYER

Oh Lord ...
Give me eyes to see Your Glory
Oh Lord ...
Give me speech to tell of Your wonders
Oh Lord ...
Give me a heart that's strong
And full of love for others

Oh Lord ...
Give me an appreciation for
The food that nourishes my body
The clothing that I wear
And thankfulness for the shelter of my home

Oh Lord ...
For all good things I thank You
And ask that You may grant me
A measure of joy in the service of others
For in giving shall I receive
And in loving shall I be loved

Take away ...
All thoughts of self
That pain may be removed
All strife and discord
That I may find peace of mind
Give me contentment in what I have
That suffering arising from selfishness may disappear

Oh Lord ...
Caring for others will I find
A Care You only can give
Take from me my sickness
That I may receive Your Love.

PRAYER FOR THE REMOVAL OF DOUBTS *

Oh God!
Out of your Mercy seek me
That I may come to You
Attract me with your Compassion
That I might turn to You

Oh God!
Though I be disobedient may I
Never lose hope in You
Nor ever cease to tremble
Even when I obey You

Oh God!
All the worlds of Creation
Have driven me to You
And knowledge of your Blessings
Has made me stand before You

Oh God!
Can I ever be disappointed when
My hope resides in You
Or ever be forsaken when
My trust is placed in You?

Oh You!
Who are veiled in the garments of your Glory
That no eye may ever see You

Oh You!
Who shines in Majestic Splendour
That mystic hearts may perceive You

Oh You!
Who does ever Manifest
How hidden can You be?

Oh You!
Who are the Eternal watching Presence;
Can You ever absent be?

* 'Abd Alla-h Abu Isma-'1-l al- 'Ansra-r1-, (died 1089).

PRAYER FOR WORLD HARMONY

Oh my Lord!

Assister of all beings

Enable all the peoples of the earth

To find Your Paradise of Faith

Let no created being remain beyond

The bounds of Your court

Or stay outside Your good pleasure

From time without beginning

Until time without end

So have You been able to do

Whatsoever You pleased and

To choose whomsoever You wished

Transcendent is Your Will above all others.

DEDICATION PRAYER

Into Your hands I commend my spirit

Lord of my Life take hold of my soul

The path You have chosen's the one I shall follow

Your Will to become my will that I may be whole

My body a vehicle to carry Your Purpose

My mind a blank slate upon which You may write

My soul and my spirit by You to be moulded

Emptied of self I am filled with Your Light.

PRAYER FOR SELFLESSNESS *

Oh God, make me a hollow reed

From which the pith of self has blown

Make me a channel of Your Love

To flow through me to all humanity.

PRAYER FOR
SELF-SUFFICIENCY IN GOD *

Say God suffices

All things above all things;

Nothing in the heavens,

Or on the earth, but God, suffices.

Verily, He is in Himself,

The Knower,

The Doer,

The Purposer,

The Sustainer,

The Omnipotent.

* Based on prayers of Ba-b Sayyid 'Al1- Muhammad ash-Shiraz1- (died 1850), some of whose followers were later to form the Baha-'1- religion.

PRAYER FOR SELF-ABANDONMENT

Oh Lord ...

> *To You do I come as my refuge*
> *Towards Your seat do I set my face*
> *Within Your precincts do I place my heart*

Oh Lord ...

> *Whether travelling or at home*
> *In my occupation or in my rest*
> *My whole confidence and trust is in You*

Oh Lord ...

> *Grant me I pray your Assistance*
> *To be independent of all but You*
> *Will that I may be satisfied*
> *With whatsoever You may ordain*

Oh Lord ...

> *Unsurpassed is Your Mercy unfailing*
> *For You are the only Decider*
> *Absolute within Your Self and able to command.*

PRAYER FOR DETACHMENT FROM THE WORLD *

Oh God who is our Lord:
Open our inner eye to illuminate
> *secrets and hidden parts,*
To extinguish all reliance on our self,
That our subsistence may be in You
> *and not within ourselves.*

* Abu-l-Abba-s Ahmad al-Murs1- (died 1287).

PILGRIMAGE PRAYER *

Used by Baba and his disciples when visiting the tombs of Sufi Saints, or the Holy places of any of the World's religions.

Oh Lord God!

Here I am at your service

(to be repeated 3 times)

You who have no partner!

Here I am at your service,

To You belongs all Praise,

For Your Bounty and Sovereignty,

Oh Lord God - my Beloved,

None can your partner be!

PRAYER FOR SEEKING REFUGE IN GOD IN TIMES OF TEMPTATION *

Oh Most Kind!

I seek refuge in You;

From the knowledge that brings no good,

From the heart that does not fear You,

From the prayer that cannot be answered,

From the self that can never be satisfied.

PRAYER FOR LIVING *

Praise be to You Oh True God!
Light of the heaven and earth,
Praise be to You Oh True God!
Guardian of heaven and earth,
Praise be to You Oh True God!
Sovereign of heaven and earth.

True are You to your promises,
True is our meeting with You,
True are the blessings of Paradise,
True is the state of anguish,
True are Your Prophets and Messengers,
True my surrender to You!

Only in You do I have faith,
Only on You do I rely,
Only your Help is unstinting,
Only to You do I turn,
Only your Mercy restores me,
Only Your Judgement is just.

For that which I do,
For that I defer,
For that I conceal,
For that I reveal,
For omissions, which You only know,
Oh True God, forgive me!

You who Expedites,
You who Defers,
You who Creates,
You who Destroys,
No other exists other than You,
You are the Source of All that You do!

67

PRAYER SAID BEFORE SLEEPING, OR WHEN ARISING FROM BED *

Oh You who are THE God!
In Your Name do I die then live again,
Blessed is the coming of death,
Praise be to You who revives me,
Raise me from death to life;
Praise be to You Oh The God!
To You is the final return.

PEACE PRAYER *

Oh Kind Lord!
You are the Author of Peace,
From You comes Peace,
And to You does Peace return;
Let us live in Peace,
May we reside in Your house of Peace:
Blessed and Exalted are You,
Oh Lord of Glory and Honour,
Hear us Oh Lord and
Grant us the pardon of Peace,
To You, may we, peacefully return.

* Inspired by and based upon prayers of the Prophet Muhammad.

A SIMPLE PRAYER *

Lord, make me an instrument of Your Peace
Where there is hatred ... let me sow Love
Where there is injury ... Pardon
Where there is discord ... Unity
Where there is doubt ... Faith
Where there is error ... Truth
Where there is despair ... Hope
Where there is sadness ... Joy
Where there is darkness ... Light

Oh Divine Master, grant that I may not so much seek
To be consoled ... as to Console
To be understood ... as to Understand
To be loved ... as to Love

For
It is in giving ... that we Receive
It is in pardoning ... that we are Pardoned
It is in dying ... that we are born to Eternal Life.

*St. Francis of Assisi

69

A MODEL PRAYER *

Oh Heavenly God and Creator of all

May we revere Your Name in all its forms

That Love may bring a Paradise to Earth

We thank You for supplying all our needs

But let not those needs be a temptation

To us to take more than our share

Help us to see the faults of others

As our own faults

That Your Kingdom may spread

From our hearts throughout the world

For You are our Source

Our Life and

Our Power

So be it.

* A prayer of Master Yesua, also known as Prophet Isa, and Jesus the Christ or Messiah.

A MORNING PRAYER

I awake refreshed in spirit
Mind and body rested now
As I breathe the morning stillness
Slowly light comes breaking through
Now a New Day has begun
Let it be a day of service
Give me joy in work and home
Let me not forget Your Kindness
Spreading Peace and Love and Light
Fill my minutes and my hours
Bring me to a peaceful night.

UNITY PRAYER *

Oh Source of our end
And of our beginning,
From whom we come
And to whom we return;
Bring us ever closer into
Your circle of Unity,
That we may rejoice with all beings:
Those that were, those that are,
And those that will be;
For You are our Life,
Our Love and our Power:
So be it!

* This prayer may also be used for the dead.

PRAYER OF GRATITUDE

All Wise and Merciful Lord
Who knows the end from the beginning
We give You thanks for Your Messengers

We who have felt the manifestation of
Your Power within our lives
Your Love within our hearts and
Your Light within our minds
Humbly submit to Your Guidance and Will

Oh Gracious Lord
Let us be Your hands and Your feet
That all may come to know You as you are
That they might enter the temple of Your service
Through the GATE of self-sacrifice
Blessed be Your many Names

Rejecting that which causes strife and division
We learn to love all beings
As Your own True Self
This is our offering to You
The Source of all that is
On this day now and for evermore.

PRAYER FOR THE REALISATION OF GOD *

Say all creation – "God is but One!"

Truth is the name of all He's creating

Without fear is He and harmful to none

Beyond births and deaths He cannot die

Realised by kindness His Self is illumined

His Name is invoked for He does not lie

True in the beginning before time commenced

True in the future and true in the now

Say all creation – "God is but One!"

INVOCATION FOR UNITY *

Say, "God is One!"

Creating all

But created by none,

Say, "God is One!"

* Inspired & based on the hymns of *Bābā* (Guru) Nanak (died 1539), founder of the Sikhs.

PRAYER FOR COMMUNITY GATHERINGS

Let us be together

Let us eat together *

Let us speak truth together

Let us radiate the Eternal Light of Life together;

Let us never speak hatred

Let us never reject anyone

Let us never cause strife or division

Let us see the One in all:

Let us not entertain the negative darkness

Which is Evil and Death.

* It is customary for Baba's followers to eat when meeting.

MARRIAGE PRAYER *

My love for thee is as a fire,
A burning passion none can quell;
My devotion is as Heaven,
Though our troubles be as Hell.
My Lord a path for me has chosen,
On this Way we both shall tread;
My companion for a lifetime,
Lover now and after death.
My remembrance and my sorrow,
Sharing joy and sharing pain;
Chronicler of deeds and actions,
Told by you I live again.
Birds of love we sit together,
Perched upon the Tree of Life,
In the service of my Master,
He has chosen thee for wife.

* This prayer is recommended in times of marital
disharmony and may also be used as a prayer during the
marriage ceremony. It expresses the devotion of those
faithful women who were partners to the **Great Teachers:**
such as Radha (wife of Krishna); Mary Magdalene
(companion of Jesus); Khadījah (wife of Muhammad) –
and who were thus in turn deeply loved, serving as examples
to all married couples.

PRAYER FOR PARENTS

Heavenly Father of my spirit
Divine Mother of My earthly form
Beloved of my soul
With You do all entreat
None can deny You, dependent are all
Life transmitted in all bodies
Wisdom displayed in the mystery of mind
Beauty manifest in its multiplicity
In You do I find existence and dissolution
Grant my parents I pray, Your assistance
Cause them to rejoice in the fruits of their labour
Forgive my sins against them as they forgave mine
May I respect and honour them
As they honoured and respected me
May the mother whose arms held me as a child
In old age be supported by mine
May the father whose guidance sustained me in youth
Feel secure in my house when he's old
Let our family become a Circle of Unity
Encompassed by Mercy and Love
Enclosed within the Might of your Protection
Drawing close to each other do we draw near to You
Source of Life, of Love and of Well-Being
Beloved of all souls from generation unto generation.

CHILDREN'S PRAYER *

Father of all, I am but a little child.
Let me be a twinkling star in
The Heaven of Your Mercy:
As a candle in the night of darkness and gloom,
A sweet singing bird perched upon the Tree of Life,
A fragrant flower in Your Garden of Delights,
An angel flying in the Paradise of Love.
By honouring my parents and listening to my teachers;
May I radiate the warmth of the Sun,
Reflect the light of the Moon,
Refresh like the morning dew,
Blossom as a rose bud;
And touch the hearts of all I meet,
That they may be
As little children
In Your Circle of Unity.
God bless all
And God bless me.

* Also used for the child's *Presentation to the Community* or *Naming Ceremony* (between 40-120 days).

A CHILD'S MEALTIME PRAYER

For the plants on the plates on our table,
For the animals who sacrificed their lives,
For the farmers in fields that planted,
For the fishermen who sail the seas,
For the cook that prepared our food,
And for God who gives us Life:
We now give thanks!

Recited by a child whilst the participants link hands before
the commencement of a meal.

PRAYER FOR MEALTIMES

Oh God who is our Father!
Oh Earth that is our Mother!
All creatures look to You for life,
Our sisters and our brothers:
Help us to see that Heaven,
Is caring for each other;
Oh let us learn to share Oh Lord,

For the peace of all the world!

Sung or recited together in unison whilst holding hands,
before or after a meal.

PRAYER FOR THE CELEBRATION OF A BIRTH

Source of Life from whom all things arise,
The One through whom all Life does multiply,
Praising You we see the origins of self:
Our sickness and our death,
Contrasted by our health.

Nothing comes forth that does not yet return,
Our death the reason for our births,
In this and endless known and unknown worlds:
Oh True God of a one and thousand names,
Our life is Yours!
Our purposes, Your aims!

So may we guide this life entrusted to us,
To help her/him grow
And to unfold until fulfilment:
We praise and celebrate this birth among us,
And see it is an individual aspect,
Of Your One Eternal Self:
Praise be to You!
Whose Love gives back to us our Self.

A prayer said at birth, or during the child's *Presentation to the Community Ceremony*. Also used when accepting an adult member into the Fraternity after taking the *Initiation vow*.

PRAYER FOR A FRIEND

Lord of Life
Who all things does control
From whom none can escape
Master of all souls
Look kindly on Your servant now
My friend who needs Your aid
And grant that s/he may know Your Love
Make his (her) spirit whole
Open his (her) heart
And clear his (her) mind
That s/he may You only see
Let him (her) glimpse Your Almighty Power
That guides his (her) destiny
Oh Lord s/he is a weary soul
Without Your Protection and Might
Help him (her) Lord to submit his (her) will
To be guided by You as right
Let him (her) not question Your Wisdom
Or seek to change Your Design
Give him (her) courage
And give him (her) hope
To follow the path Divine
Take away all fearful thoughts
Help him (her) to see Reality
To know this world as a futile place
Unless s/he You can see
Open his (her) eyes to a vision sublime
And his (her) ears to the song of Love
Give him (her) constancy
In his (her) time of need
And blessings from Heaven above.

PRAYER FOR THE DYING

All Merciful and Compassionate Lord
Give ear to our cry for solace and for peace
Gentle Master of our Fate
We beseech You now to listen
To our plea for Divine Assistance
In this our hour of need
Humbly we submit to Your Will
For You are the Source of Life
Of Being and of Existence
From You all things have their beginning
And to You do all things return
Give us courage now to face the times ahead
Knowing that in our sorrow and our grief
You are our comfort and our hope
No longer struggling within our self
We graciously accept Your Direction
The spirit cries out from the mortal flesh
Desiring to be freed from
The bondage of the material worlds
The night is dark and we wish to greet
The day before us clothed in the garments
Of peace and of tranquillity.
Good Lord, lead your servant
Into Your Light of Love
That s/he may stand with
Those who have gone before

Give us eyes to see Your Glory
And hearts full of thankfulness
For the times we shared and will share again
For in death is to be found birth
And in dying do we find Eternal Life
Oh Merciful and Compassionate Lord
We submit to Your Will
No more to struggle against the tides of Time
But allow this soul to slip
Into Your Eternal Ocean
That s/he may flow with all that is
Now and for evermore
So be it.

This prayer is said at death or shortly thereafter. All members of the immediate family recite, or chant it in unison, in the presence of the departed.

PRAYER FOR ENDURING HARDSHIP OR PERSECUTION *

All praise to You!
Oh my God;
Magnified be Your Name
Oh Beloved of my soul:
Humanity's Highest Aspiration,
Goal of all beings,
Helpmate of the poor,
Deliverer of the oppressed,
Abaser of the haughty,
Destroyer of Evil;
You are in truth the Lord
Of all Creation,
And of every Revelation.

Sufficient unto Your Self,
Yet You are my companion;
My Assistance in need,
My Delight in solitude,
My Beloved in my loneliness,
My Witness in my affliction,
My Comfort in my travail:
Never shall I grieve,
For in You I put my trust,

Even though I die*
I shall not perish;
Though I be ridiculed,
I shall not be put to shame.

Whosoever puts their trust in You
Shall not be disappointed,
Whatsoever You desire,
This shall come into being;
Even as Your creation
Which has never ceased
Nor ever shall.
Whatsoever is written
For me in Your Book,
That I will follow;
For You are in truth,
The Lord of Power and Glory:
Master of all worlds.

* Inspired by all those who have sacrificed their life for Truth.

A SUFI PRAYER *

Oh God!
Pardon my lack of sincerity
In asking forgiveness from Thee
May I take refuge in You
From all that distracts from Thee
Grant my heart Your Presence
That I may remember Thee
Let my wish in this world be Your work
That my prayers be not empty.

May my satisfaction reside
In whatsoever You Will for me
If I worship Thee out of fear
Let that fear devour me
If I have hope of reward
May I be excluded from Thee
Let me serve You for Your own sake
This is sufficient for me.

For You are my joy and my longing
And Ultimate Destiny
My Friend who desires my welfare
And provides me sanctuary
You are my spirit and hope
My life and vitality
Through all the Worlds of Existence
I've wandered in search of Thee.

You are my heart's Commander
That causes my eyes to shine
Thy Gracious gifts unending
And Your Merciful Bounties Divine
I am blessed in Your service
May I never be free
Oh God, my heart's desire
        Be satisfied with me!

* Inspired by prayers of Rābi'ah al-'Adawiyya.

PRAYER OF REPENTANCE

Oh Loving One:

I am weak

    but You are Strong

I am poor

    but You are Rich

I am lowly

    but You are Noble

I am sorrowful

    but You are full of Joy

I am pitiful

    but You are the Source of Majesty

I am foolish

    but You are Wisdom itself

I am ignorant

    but You are Knowledge unceasing

I am dependent

    but You are Powerful

I am sickly

    but You are Life in fullness

I am mortal

    but You are without beginning or end

I am a part

    but You are the Whole

I am sinful

    but You are Holy

Oh Master of Destiny:

Look not at my strength

  but see my weakness

Pitiful am I

  forever dependent on Your Mercy

May I no longer be sorrowful

  but rise up to be assisted

By Your Power and Majesty

  To do great things in Your Name

Spreading Your Truth

  do I become wise

Trusting in You

  do I become rich

    in the knowledge of all things

Sharing Your Love

  I am a joyful being

Unharassed by negative thoughts

  I become a Physician to all

Assisted by Your Spirit

  I am a whole being

Detached from suffering and sin

  I become a messenger wholly

Engaged in serving You:

  Now and for evermore.

PRAYERS FOR FASTING

Oh my God! Oh my Lord! Oh my Master!*
I beseech Your forgiveness
For seeking any pleasure but Your love
For desiring any comfort except Your nearness
For searching for any delight
Other than Your good-pleasure
For any existence at all except communion with You.

Praise be to You! Praise be to You!
Oh my Lord, forgive us our shortcomings
Have Mercy upon us and assist us
To return to You and Your Path
Enable us to rely on You
Assure us of Your Goodness and Might
By allowing us to return to You

Exalted be the station
Of those who truly believed,
May they be to us an example of Your Mercy
You are our Help in all things
The self-subsistent
Desiring nothing but our well-being.

Magnified be Your Name, Oh Lord our God!
You are in truth the Knower of things unseen
Destine that which in Your inestimable Wisdom
Is for our best measure
Yours is the Sovereignty and the Dominion

You are the Best Beloved.

* This line to be repeated *at least* 3 times.

ESKIMO PRAYER *

I asked God for strength so I might achieve

I was made weak that I might learn to obey

I asked for health to do great things

I was given infirmity so I might do better things

I asked for riches that I might be happy

I was given poverty in order to become wise

I asked for power to have the praise of men

I was given weakness so as to feel the need of God

I asked for all these things to enjoy my life

I got nothing that I asked for

But everything I had hoped for

Despite my desires - my self -

Unspoken prayers were answered

Now amongst all men and women

I am so very richly blessed.

* Based upon a prayer used by *Nana* Layla Karman (Baba's wife) and acquired through her association with an Alaskan spiritual teacher.

HEBREW PRAYER *

The Lord Eternal is my shepherd
So nothing do I lack
In green meadows does He make me lie
Beside peaceful waters leads me
Life He renews within me
And in His name guides me in the right path

Even though I walk through death's dark valley
Evil I do not fear for You are with me
Your staff and Your crook are my comfort
In the sight of my enemies
You lay out a table for me
My head with oil You have anointed
And my cup is over-filled

Surely Goodness and Love never failing
Will follow me always
And in the dwelling-place of You MY LORD
Shall I stay all the days of my life.

* Rendering of Psalm 23 from the **Holy Bible**.

DRUID PRAYER

Grant, O God, Thy protection
And in protection, strength;
And in strength, understanding;
And in understanding, knowledge;
And in knowledge, the knowledge of justice;
And in the knowledge of justice, the love of it;
And in the love of it, the love of all existence;
And in the love of all existence, the love of God:
God and all Goodness.

SANSKRIT PRAYER *

Oh Lord, may we feel that
You are the Soul of souls;
May our bodies be Your home,
May everything that we enjoy
Be an offering to You:
May our every word be a hymn to You,
Our every act Your adoration,
Our every step a pilgrimage to Your Shrine.
May we see the world as lit by Your Light;
May we know You as our beginning,
May we know You as our end,
Oh Omni, (AUM-NEE) You are our own True Self.

* Based upon a traditional Hindu prayer.

CHINESE PRAYER *

I am but a flower lost in a garden of weeds
... This I know
I am but a garden of weeds lost in a large town
... This I know
I am but a large town lost in a vast country
... This I know
I am but a country lost in the sea
... This I know
I am but a sea lost in an Ocean of raindrops
... This I know
I am but a raindrop lost in a shower
... This I know
I am but a shower washing the face of a flower
... This I know
I am but a flower lost in a garden of weeds
... This I know

I am nothing but that which is lost
And lost do I find myself
Oh may I always lose myself in what I do
That I may know my real True Self
Then I will know that you are I
And I am You.

* Inspired by the
Taoist tradition.

NORTH AMERICAN INDIAN PRAYER *

Great Sea you have set me adrift
Moved me as the weed in a river
Earth Mother and Father Weather
You have carried me away
And moved my inward parts with joy
The trees and the rocks see Your deeds
The wind whispers Your voice
Spirit of the cliff I know Your craggy face
The soaring sky that cries with birds
Warm womb of the soil with sapling springing
That nourishes the worm that from my body feeds
Great Circle of Existence timelessly turning
Turn now my thoughts to flowing
With Waterfall I drop into Ocean
And return in Springtime's rain
Great Spirit give me the courage of a mountain lion
That I may leap through life
And stand upon the Ancestral shore
Watching the Great Sea
Wash away the sands of life.

* Inspired by Great Elk, Sun Bear,
Little Turtle, and other American
Indian leaders Baba met.

AFRICAN PRAYER *

Divinity, we call You in our invocation!
You help all tribes and people
You are Great
Above all and in all
All people are Your creation

Divinity our Creator
We fear Your Power more than any man
But even though we are alone
You will not desert us
Let that which is inside us speak

Let affection and unity be among us now
And let hate depart with those who hate us
If enemies celebrate our downfall we shall not fear
For in our death we will live again
And in the dreams of others shall we return

Divinity, we call You in our prayer
That we may know You in ourselves.

* Based on prayers of the Dinka, a Sudanese tribal people.

PERSIAN PRAYER *

Wise Lord!
Give me the courage to oppose the Lie
And all that from it springs
The strength to stand and fight
When all against Thee turn
Help me to see with eagle-eye a vision pure
When all have come to Thee
No more the Evil One
To divide and rule our soul

In Ages past You came to give us Light
And come again now Earth is dark
Your Will none can defeat
Though hate may devour my body
My soul will soar aloft
To the place of Infinite Time
Consumed by the fire of devotion
I burn with zeal for right
Standing tall like a tower amidst decay
Blazing forth Thy Glory now and for evermore.

* Based on the hymns of Spitama
Zar'dustrā (Zarathustra), founder
of the Parsees and Zoroastrians.

This prayer is primarily for use by the tribal peoples of the world, in recognition of their tragic history as the result of European colonisation. Its significance lies in its prophetic nature, predicting that these people (yellow, black and red) will become the harbingers of a New World Civilisation.

A PRAYER FOR THE TRIBAL PEOPLES

Oh Spirit of Life we call upon You:
that our brothers who fly in the heavens,
our cousins who crawl upon the earth,
and our sisters who swim in its waters,
may live!
Cause to arise from amongst the people:
a mighty nation of many tongues and colours,
the visible and invisible among us,
united in our hearts, our action and our speech, to
Bless our Mother Earth!
Through suffering and struggle have You prepared us:
the red, the yellow and the black,
our blood to purify the evils of all peoples,
all beings great and small in harmony sustain us,
So give us Peace!
Grant us courage and the strength to oppose:
to resist those who oppress and exploit,
in Your Name to lie and cheat the people,
that Your limitless Mercy may be manifest
Upon us now!
Bless those who assist and aid us:
curse those who indifferently oppose us,
that the sacred Tree may give its fruit,
and the sacred Hoop be strong again,
that the spirits of our ancestors may rest in peace,
So let it be!

A PRAYER TO BEGIN THE DAY *

Said immediately after washing on arising from bed.

Thanks be to God
The Everliving King!
Who mercifully restores
My sentient soul to me
Waking from my slumbers
My spirit now returns
To You in whom all Life exists
For Whom our spirits yearn
In You we place our trust

Within me You created
A spirit that was pure
You surely formed and breathed it in
And soon will take it back
That it may be restored
So long as it remains with me
Then I shall offer thanks
Oh God, God of my fathers
Master of all souls
Blessed are You Lord
Who brings forth life from death

Guard my tongue from evil
Comparisons and deceits
My lips from speaking falsehood
Slander or conceit
Open my heart to Your Teaching
Wisdom and Your Way
May I follow your commands
As I live my life this day
Make my actions, words and thoughts
Pleasing always to You
Sole Source of my soul's satisfaction
My strength and Redeeming Truth.

PRAYER OF THANKS FOR FOOD *

Blessed are You, Oh Lord our God,
Ruler of all worlds!
Creator of every living thing and of its needs:
For that which you have created
To sustain your creatures,
Blessed are You, Oh Life of all the worlds!

HYMN TO ACKNOWLEDGE THE DIVINE UNITY *

He is the Lord Eternal!
Who ruled before all things were made;
When all was done according to His Will,
He was already then - THE King!

And after all has ceased to be,
Still will He rule alone in majesty;
He was, He is and He shall ever be,
Glorious for all eternity!

One alone is He,
None can compare or partner Him:
Without beginning and an end
All Power and Sovereignty are His!

HE IS MY God and Saviour!
My Rock in difficult distress:
He is my Guide and Refuge,
My Assister when I call on Him

Into His hands do I give my being,
Whether asleep or whether awake;
So long as life remains with my body,
The Lord will be with me and I shall not fear.

* Derived from Jewish prayers. The Hebrew on which the
Unity hymn is based is on the next page.

בְּטֶרֶם כָּל־יְצִיר נִבְרָא,   אֲדוֹן עוֹלָם, אֲשֶׁר מָלַךְ,
אֲזַי מֶלֶךְ שְׁמוֹ נִקְרָא.   לְעֵת נַעֲשָׂה בְחֶפְצוֹ כֹּל,

לְבַדּוֹ יִמְלוֹךְ נוֹרָא,   וְאַחֲרֵי כִּכְלוֹת הַכֹּל,
וְהוּא יִהְיֶה בְּתִפְאָרָה.   וְהוּא הָיָה, וְהוּא הֹוֶה,

לְהַמְשִׁיל לוֹ, לְהַחְבִּירָה,   וְהוּא אֶחָד, וְאֵין שֵׁנִי
וְלוֹ הָעֹז וְהַמִּשְׂרָה.   בְּלִי רֵאשִׁית, בְּלִי תַכְלִית,

וְצוּר חֶבְלִי בְּעֵת צָרָה,   וְהוּא אֵלִי, וְחַי גּוֹאֲלִי,
מְנָת כּוֹסִי בְּיוֹם אֶקְרָא.   וְהוּא נִסִּי וּמָנוֹס לִי,

בְּעֵת אִישָׁן וְאָעִירָה,   בְּיָדוֹ אַפְקִיד רוּחִי
יְיָ לִי, וְלֹא אִירָא.   וְעִם־רוּחִי גְּוִיָּתִי :

ADON OLAM

Adon Olam Asher Malach	B'terem Kol-Ytzir Niv'ra
L'ait Naasa V'chef'tzo Kol	Azay Melech Sh'mo Nikra
V'acharai Kich'lot Hakol	L'vado Yim'loch Nora
V'hu Haya V'hu Hoveh	V'hu Yihyehh B'tifarah
V'hu Echad V'ahyn Sheyni	L'ham'shil Lo L'hachbira
B'lee Rayshit B'lee Tach'lit	V'lo Haoz V'hamisra
V'hu Eli V'chai Goali	V'tzur Chev'li B'ayt Tzara
V'hu Nisi U'manos Li	M'anta Kosi B'yom Ek'ra
B'yad Af'kid Ruchi	B'ayat Iyshan V'aira
V'eim-Ruchi G'vyati	Adonai Li V'li Iyrah

THE BREAKING OF BREAD *

We break this bread for :-

Those who love God,
For those who follow the path of the Buddha
And worship the God of the Hindus;
For our sisters and brothers in Islam,
And for the Jewish people from whom we come.
We pray that one day we may be as one.

We break this bread for :-

The great green earth;
We call to mind the forests, fields and flowers,
Which we are destroying,
That one day,
With the original blessing,
God's creation will be restored.

We break this bread:-

For those who have no bread;
The starving,
The homeless,
And for all refugees.
That one day this planet may be a home for everyone.

We break this bread:-

For the broken parts of ourselves,
The wounded child in all of us,
For our broken relationships,
That one day we may glimpse
The wholeness that is of God's anointed.

* A prayer said at the *Breaking of the Bread Ceremony*, composed
by the Revd. Donald Reeves, former vicar of St. James Church,
Piccadilly, London. (See Acts 2:47 in the **Holy Bible**)

THE FRATERNITY OF THE UNIVERSAL WAY

Their Temple : The empty and open heart.

Their Worship : The expression of humanity
in the service of all Life.

Their Creed : Love.

Their Prophet : The Eternal Guiding Spirit.

Their Scriptures : The Sacred Book of Nature.

Their Way : Selfless Devotion.

Their Object : Perfect Joy.

"Love transcends all religions - its expression is Peace and its realisation Joy - this is my creed!"

The Universality of the message of the spiritual Master **Baba Dovid Yusuf** is expressed in the sayings, prayers and meditations he used. Jewish mystic, Ancient Egyptian Initiate, Indo-Persian Sage and teacher of Celtic wisdom, he was also an honorary member of several native tribes. Affiliated to numerous Sufi Orders, including the Central Asian **Khwājagān** (the Masters), it was these ancient teachings, *the basis of* all the world's religious traditions, that Baba preserved by his message and way of life, teaching a spirituality that transcended religious differences.

Initiating projects concerned with ecology and medicine, world peace, conservation and the rights of indigenous peoples; he guided, administered healing and encouraged: the mentally and physically disabled, convicts in prison, show-business celebrities, scientists and scholars, and even royalty. Helping others to find their way, assisting change – sometimes great – in the many people's lives he touched.

Appearing in Iran at the end of the 19th century, in India in the 20th century and later in Turkey and Cyprus – the compiler of this book was given a mandate in 1976, whilst in Israel/Palestine, to continue this work. To avoid development of a cult and not wishing to claim ownership of these Universal teachings, Baba insisted that personal details of his life are not disclosed. Though no longer in

103

the material world, he continues to influence a worldwide change in consciousness.

Proceeds from the sale and distribution of this book go to the **Rainbow (charitable) Trust** to continue this work.

INDEX

In order to facilitate its use by study groups as well as private individuals, the items in this Index have been listed under both subject and word location: i.e., the actual word may not be found under the page number given, but material relating to that subject will be found on that page. As such, it will be found to contain guidance and teachings for every facet of both personal, community and national life.

114